Fashion Corquis Book

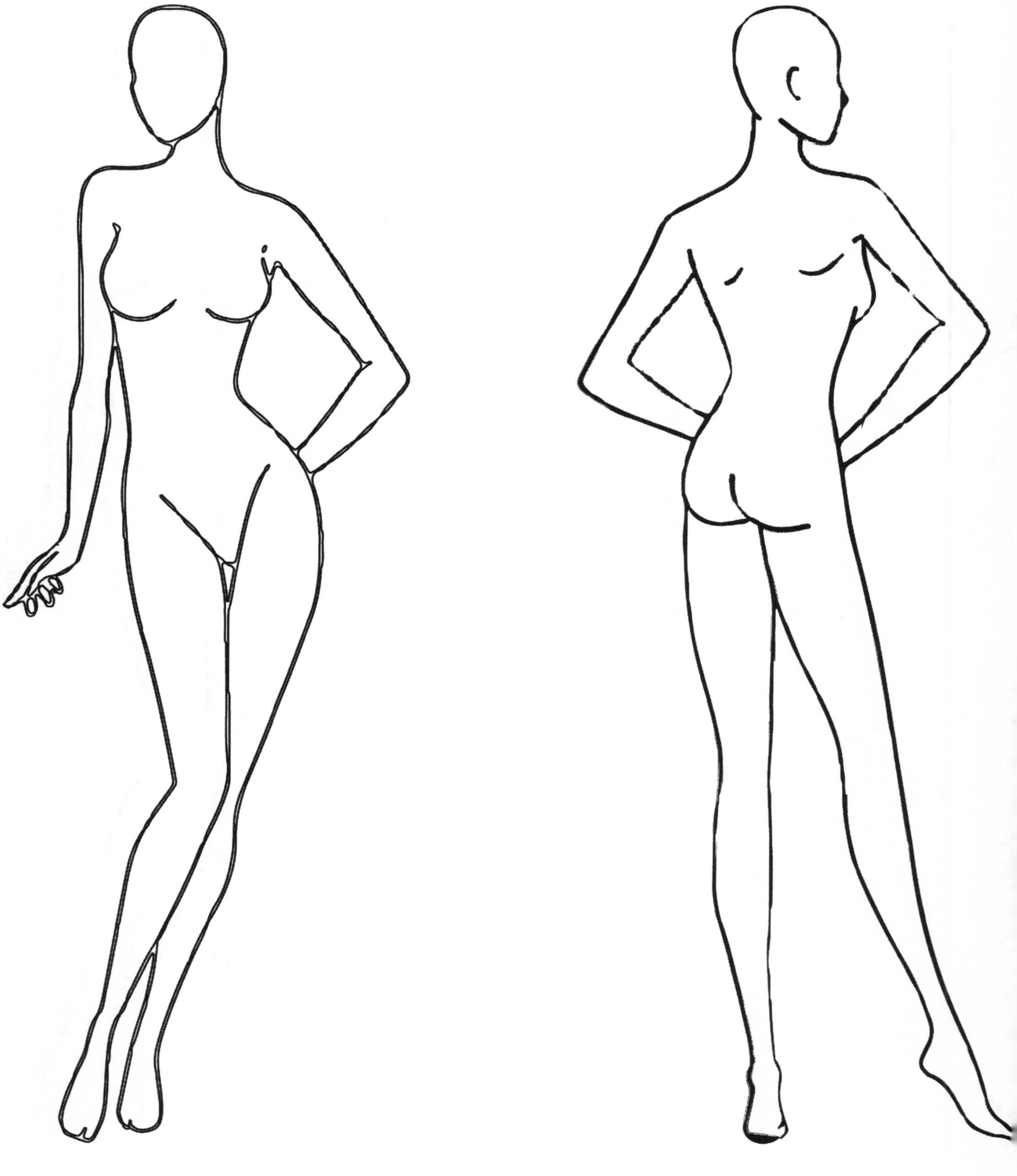

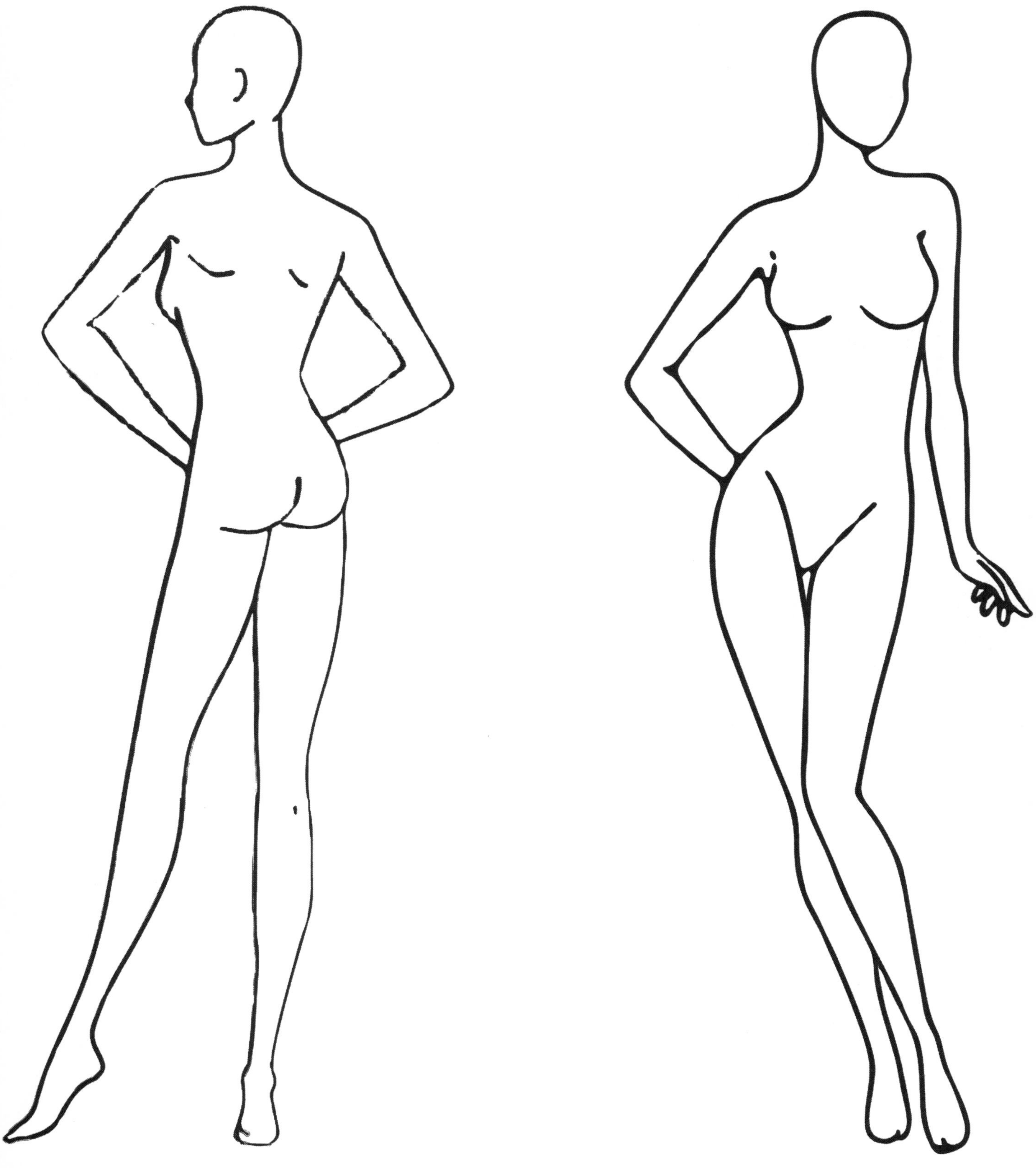

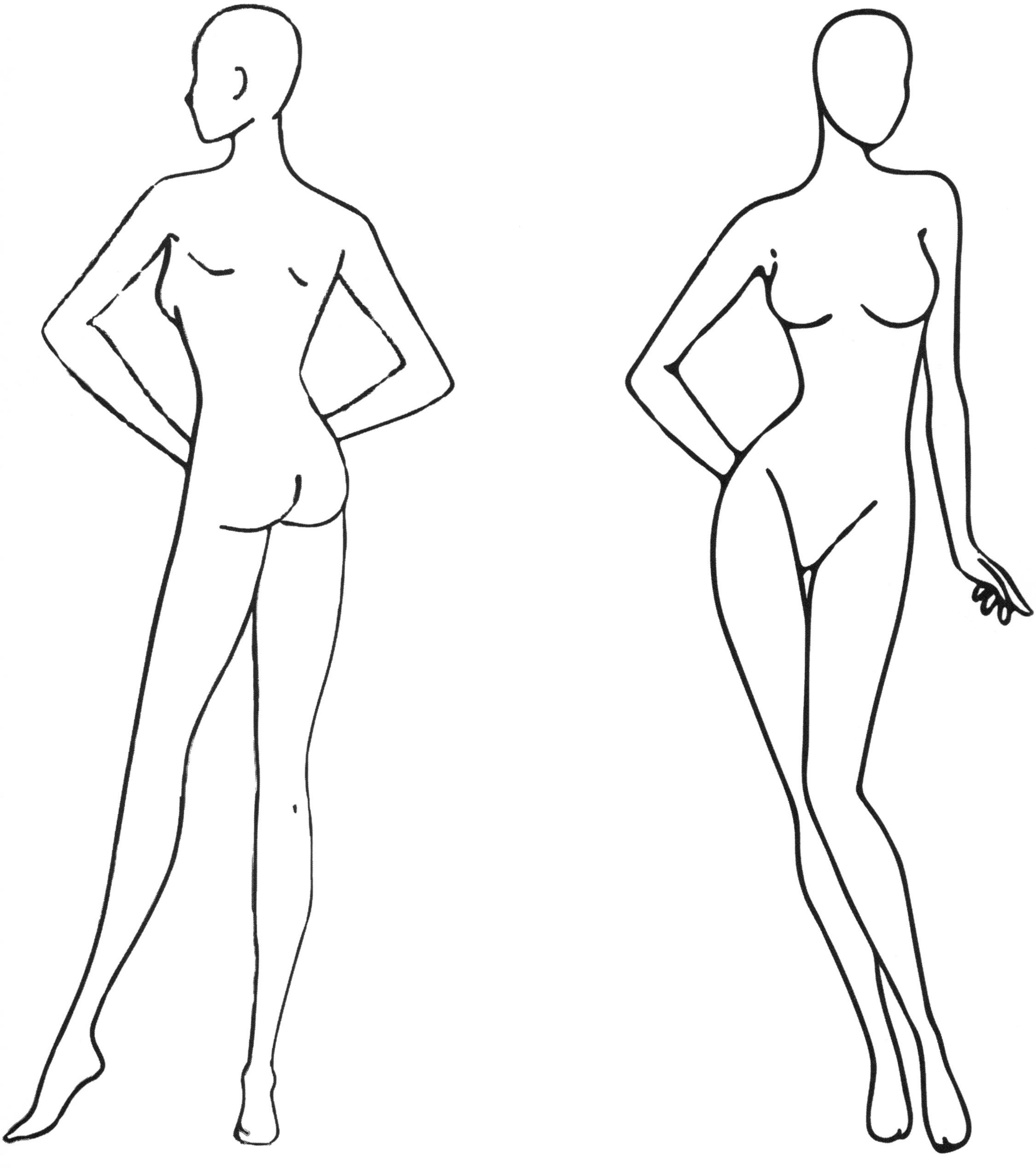

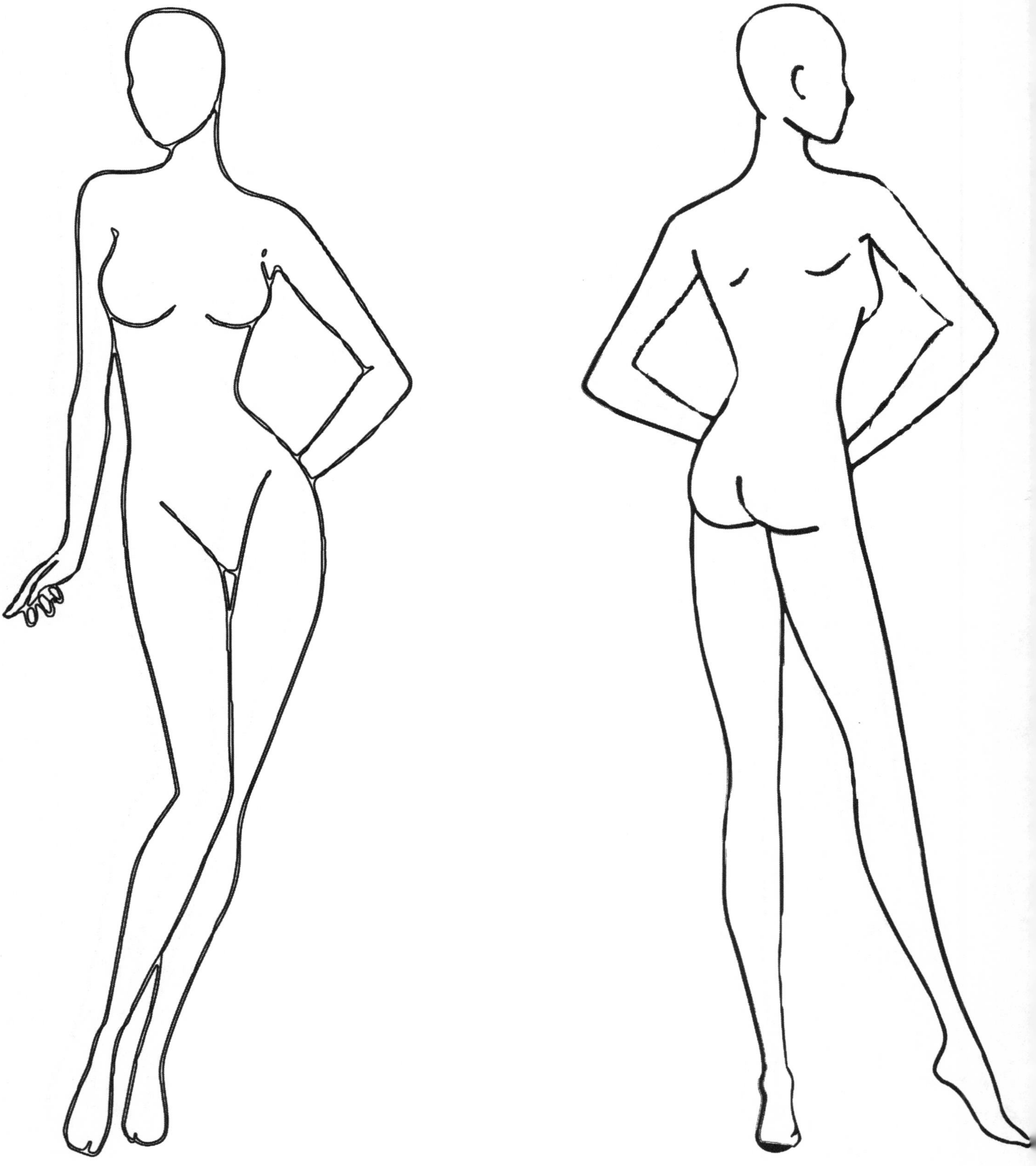

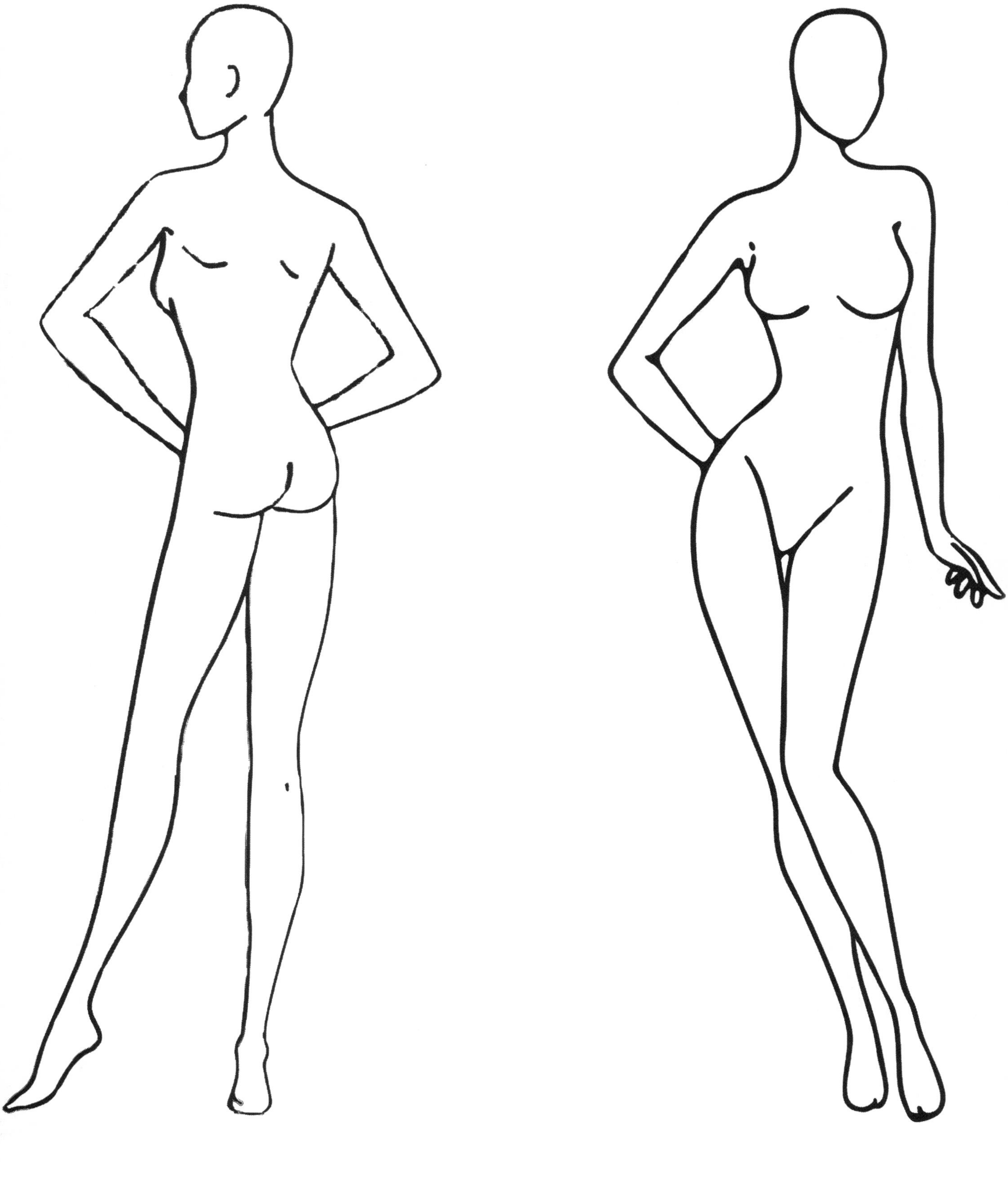

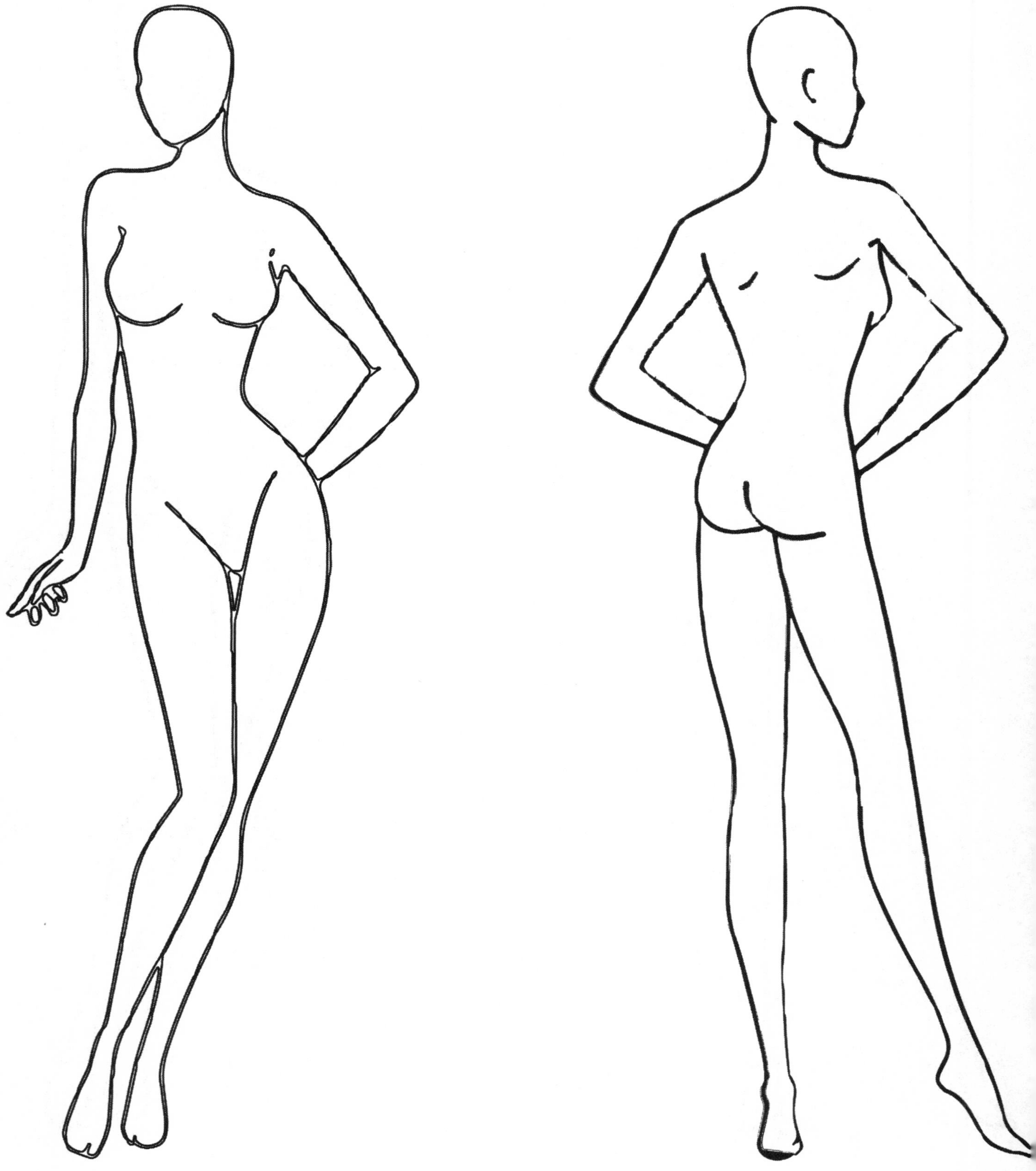

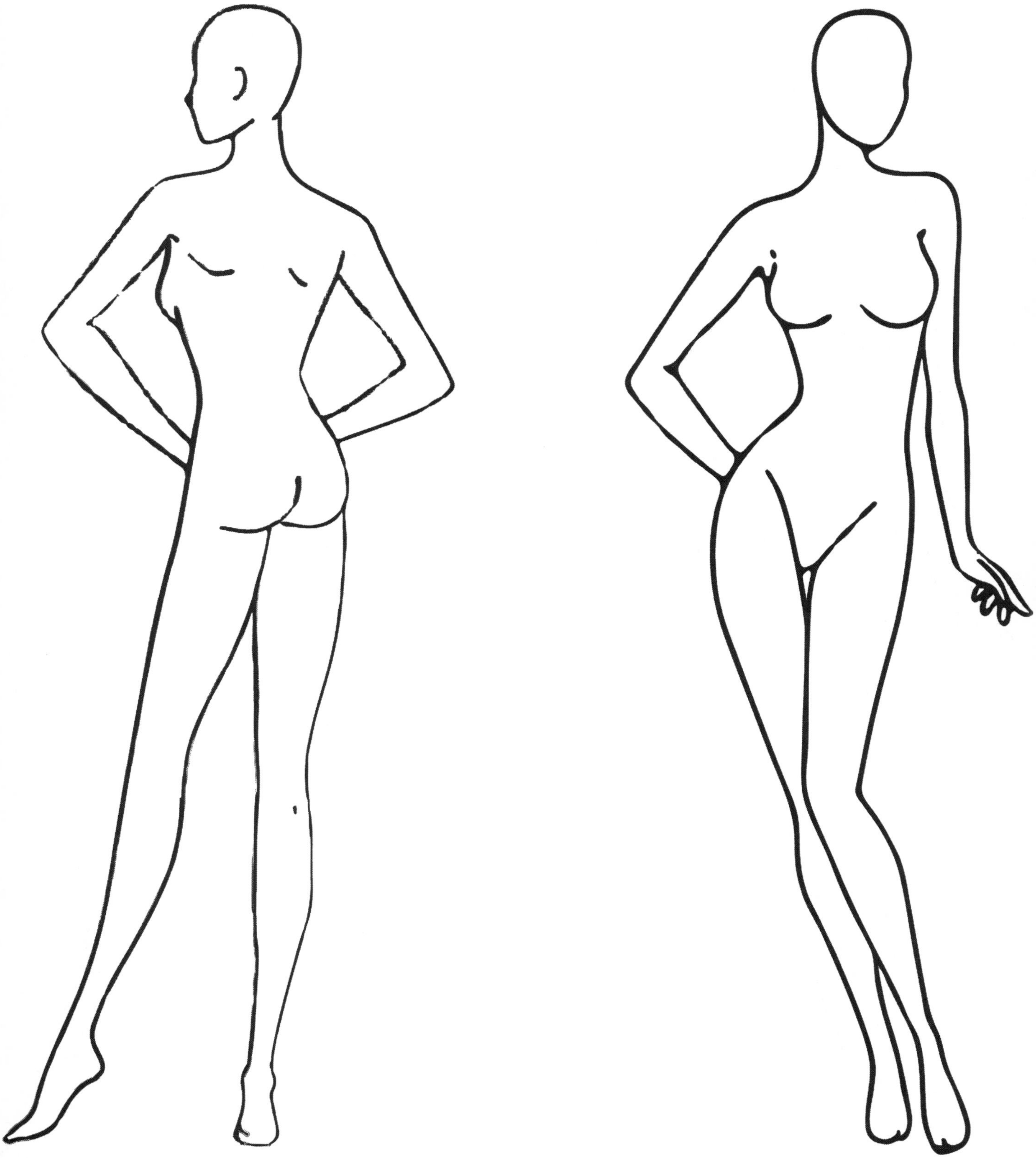

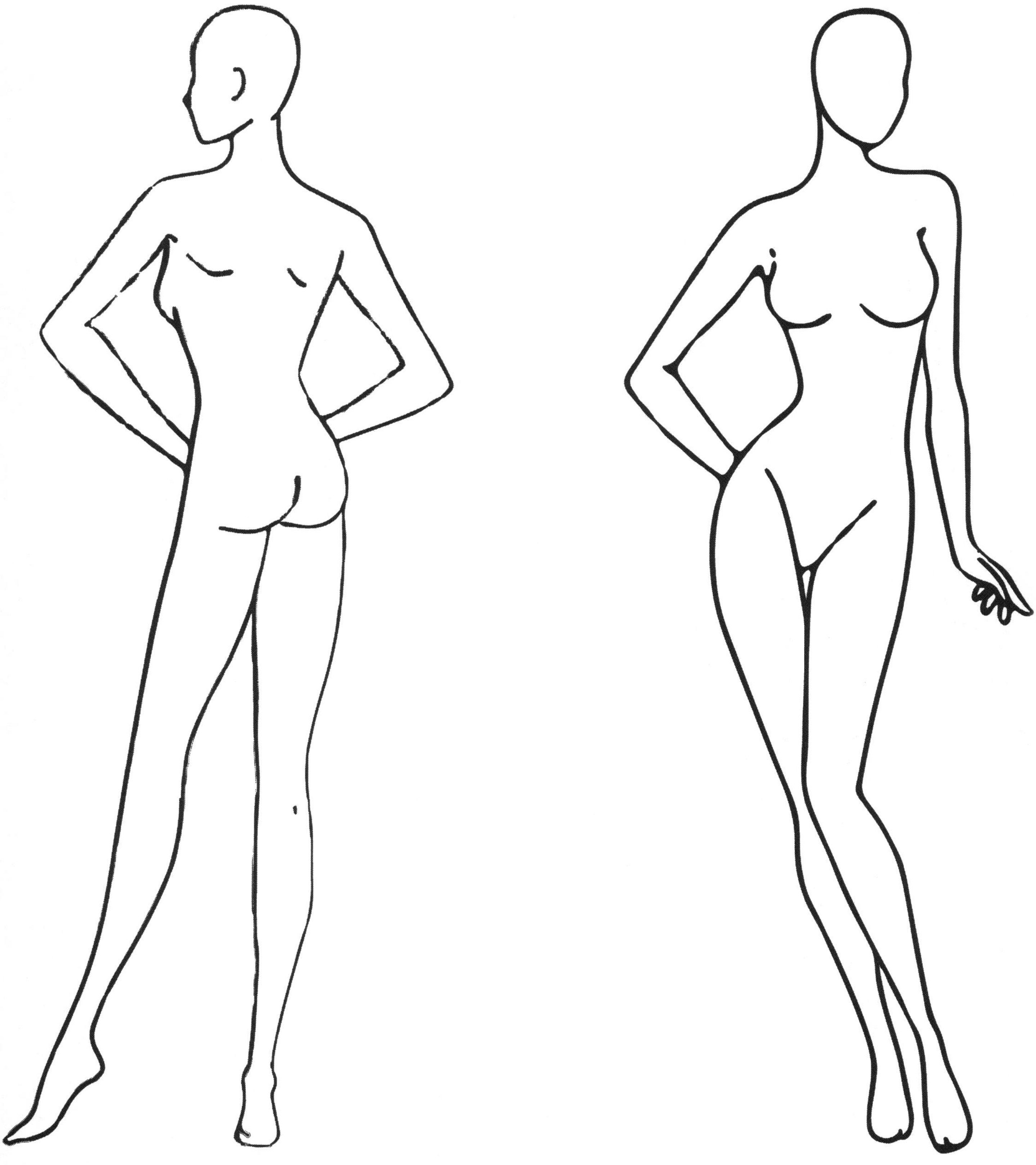

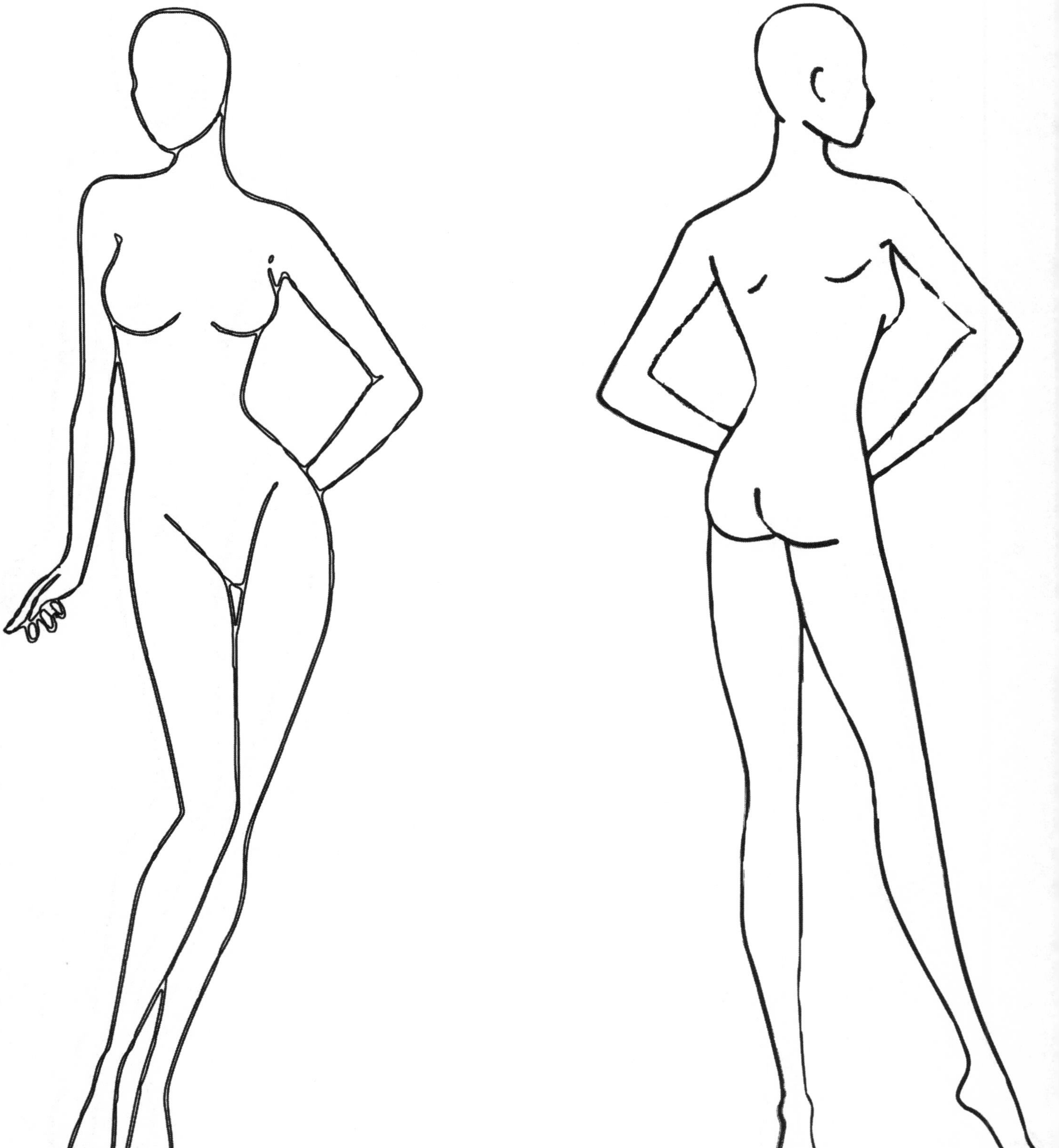

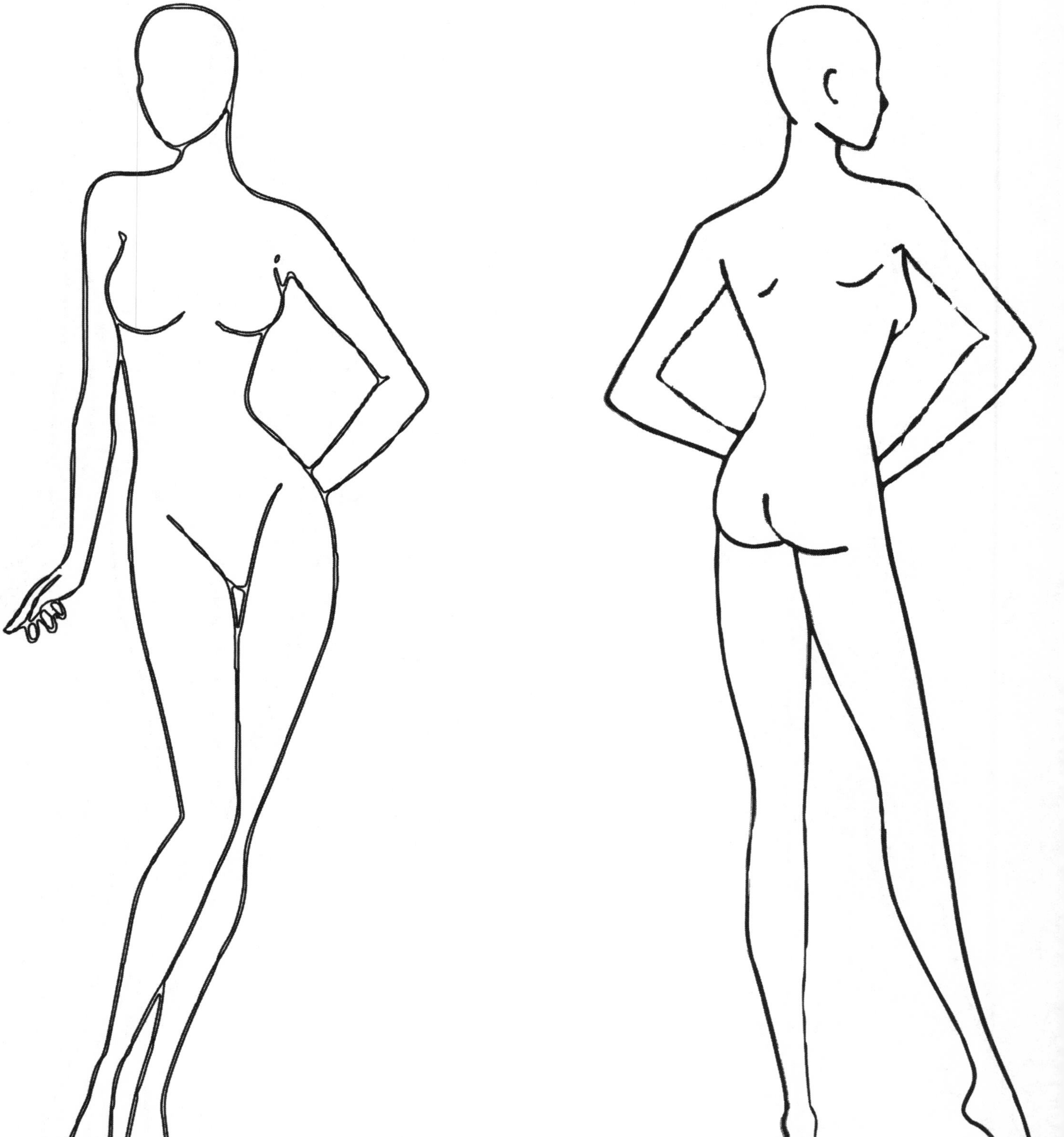

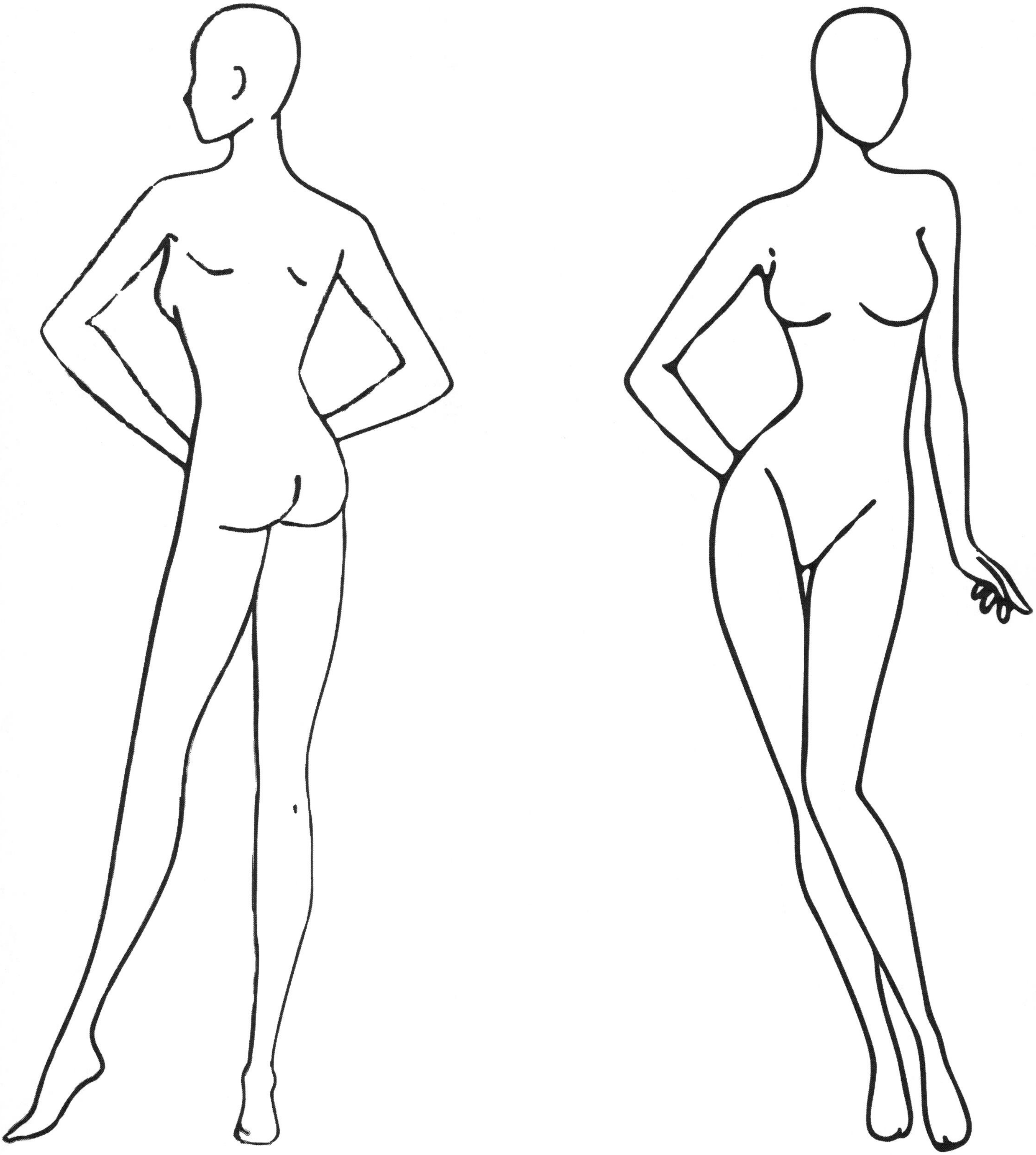

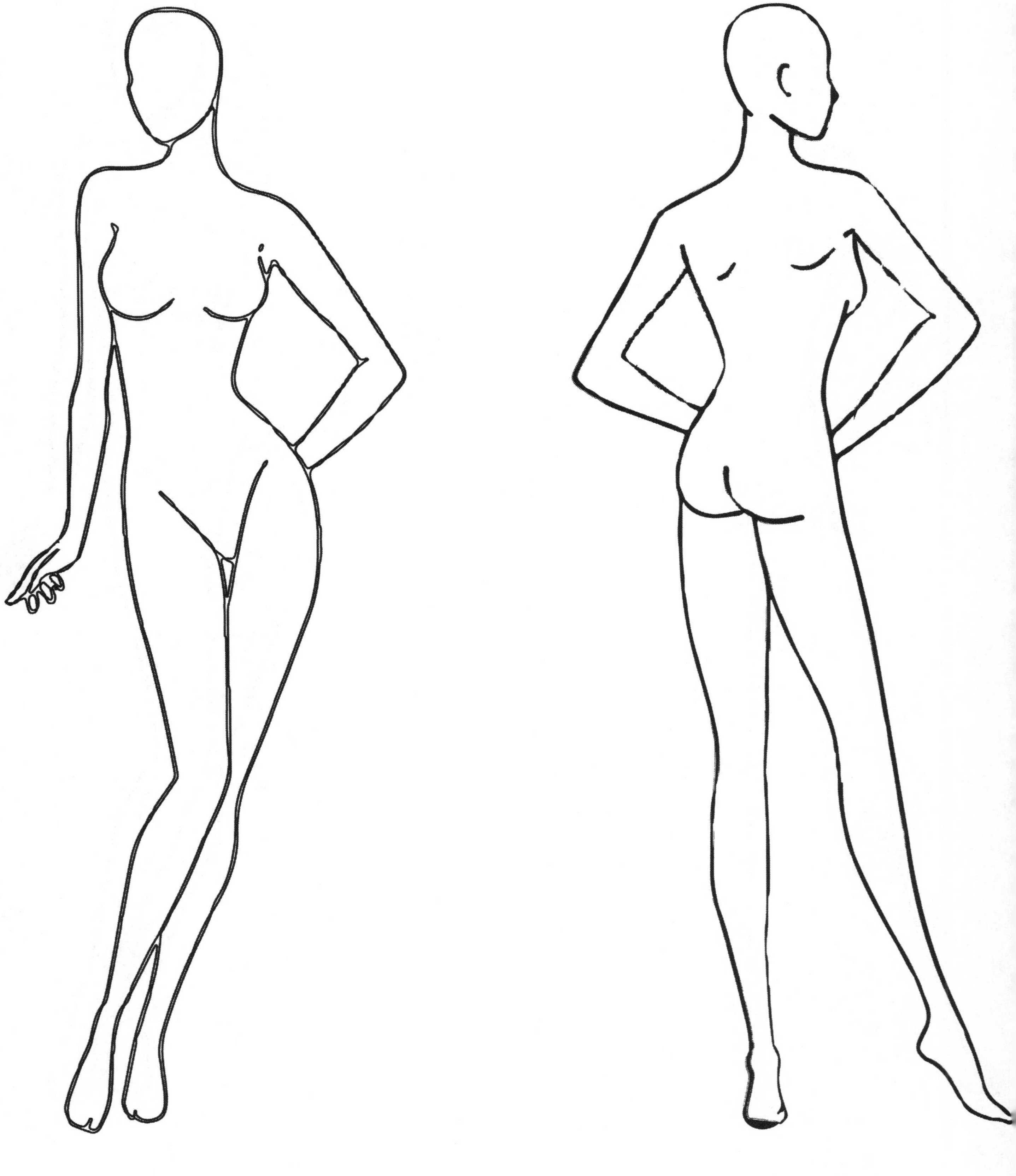

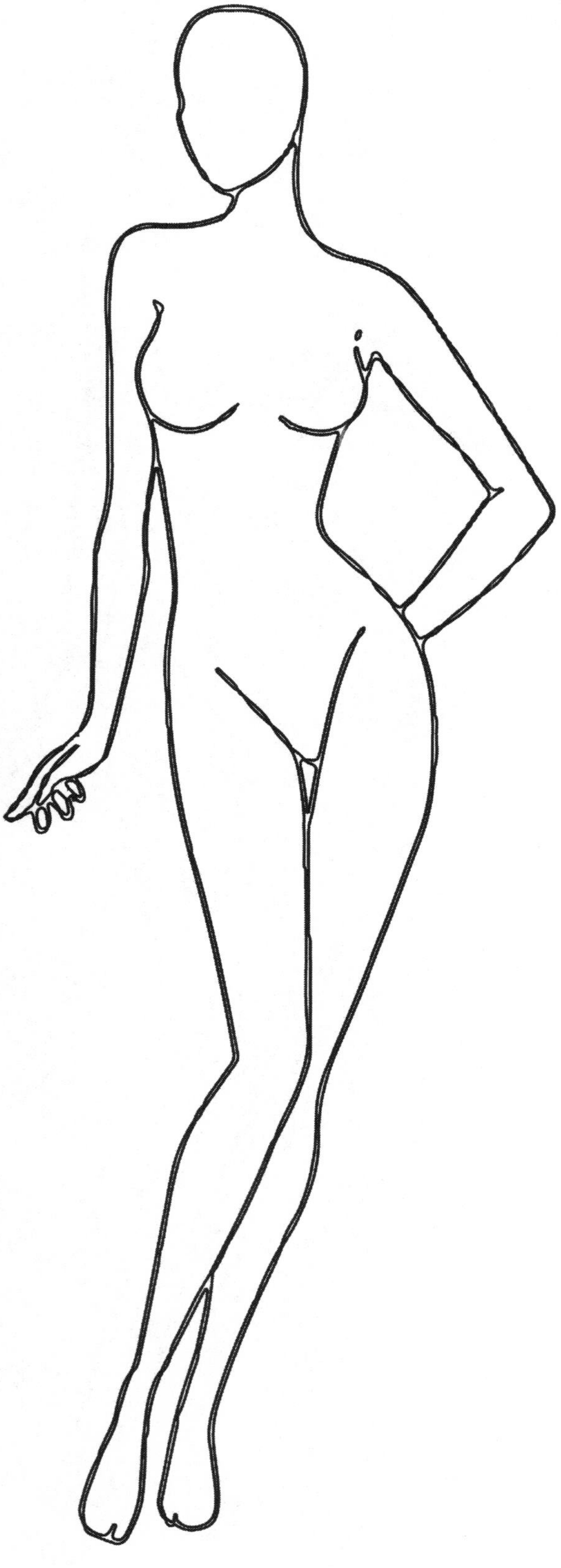

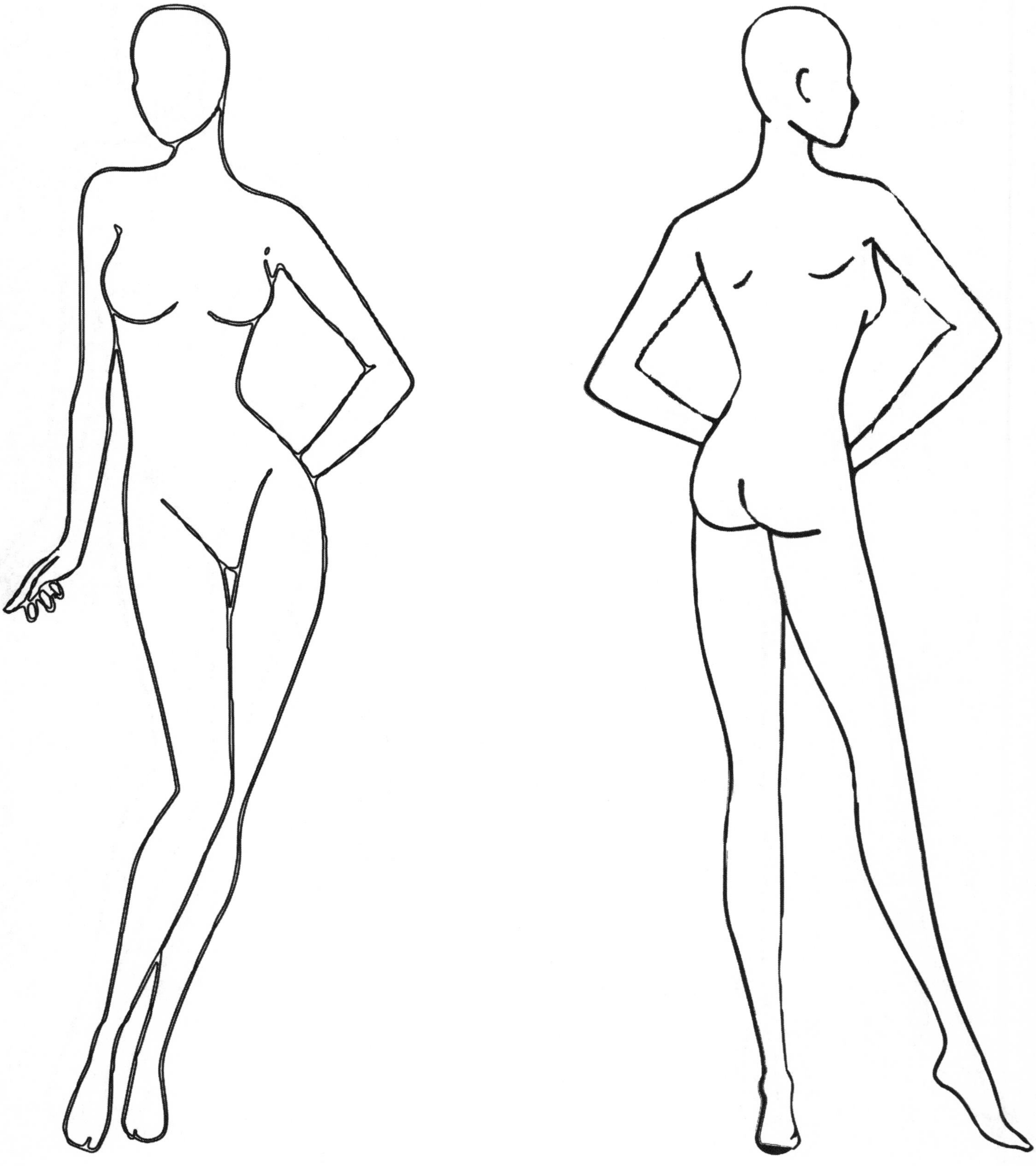

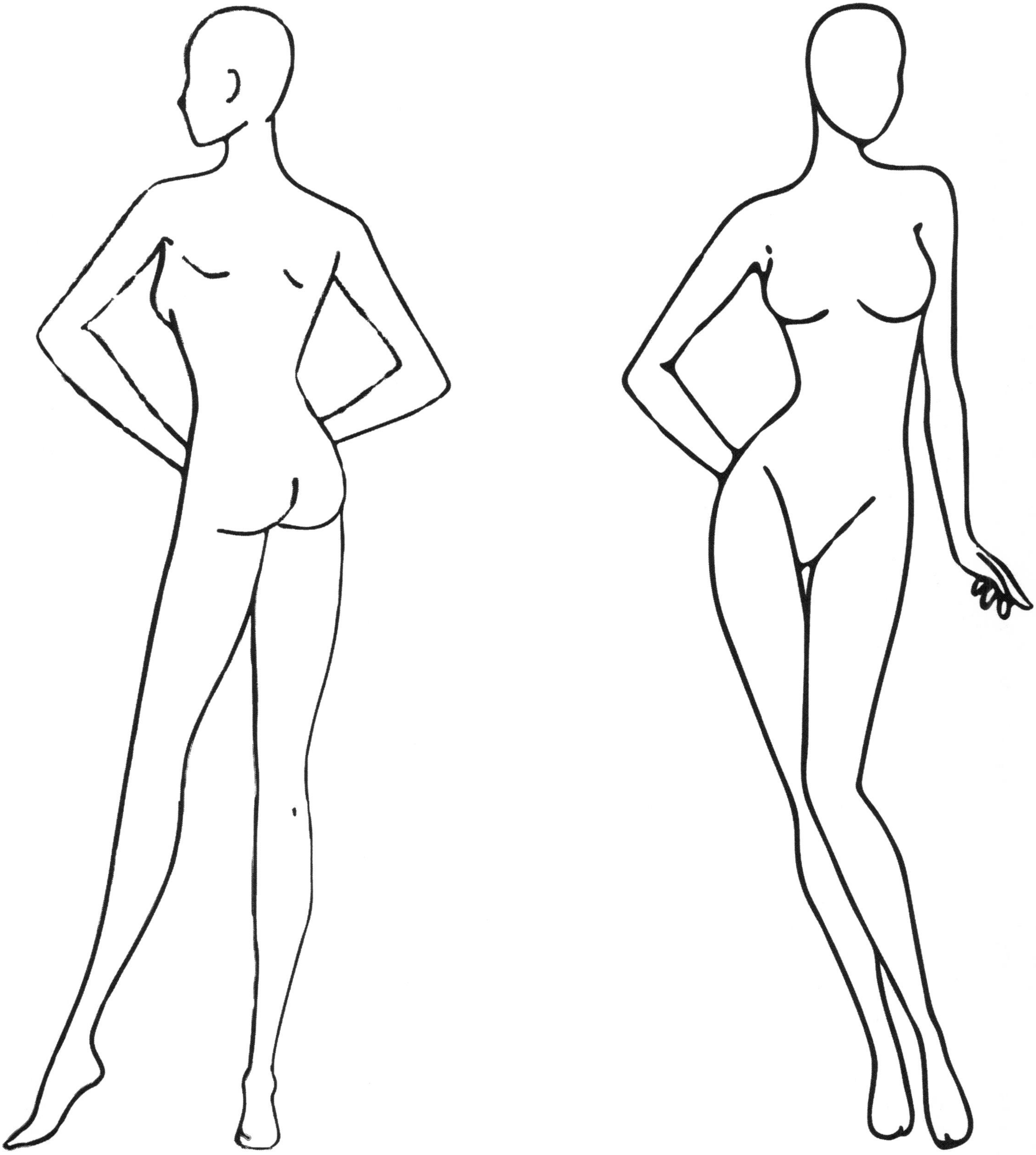

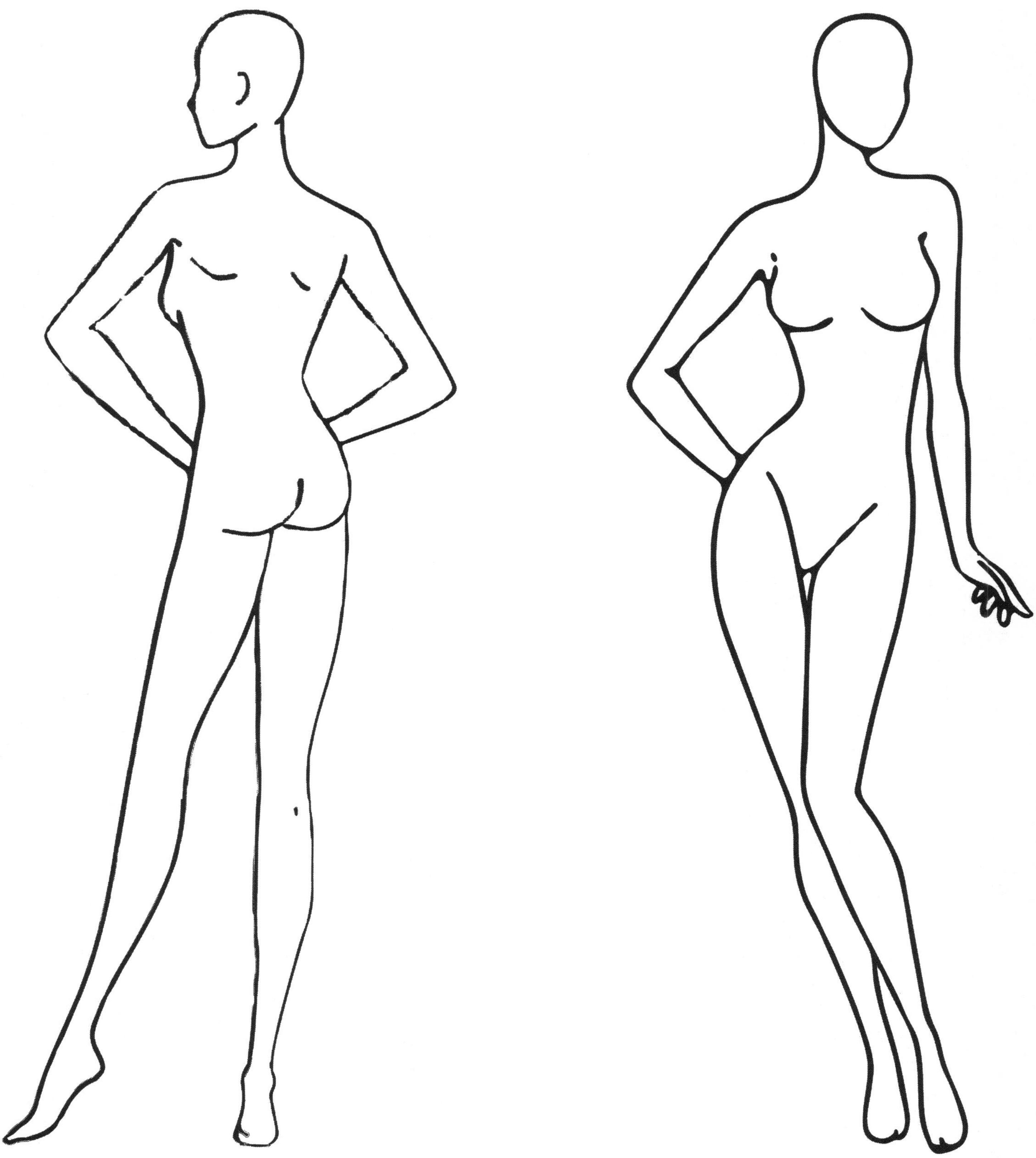

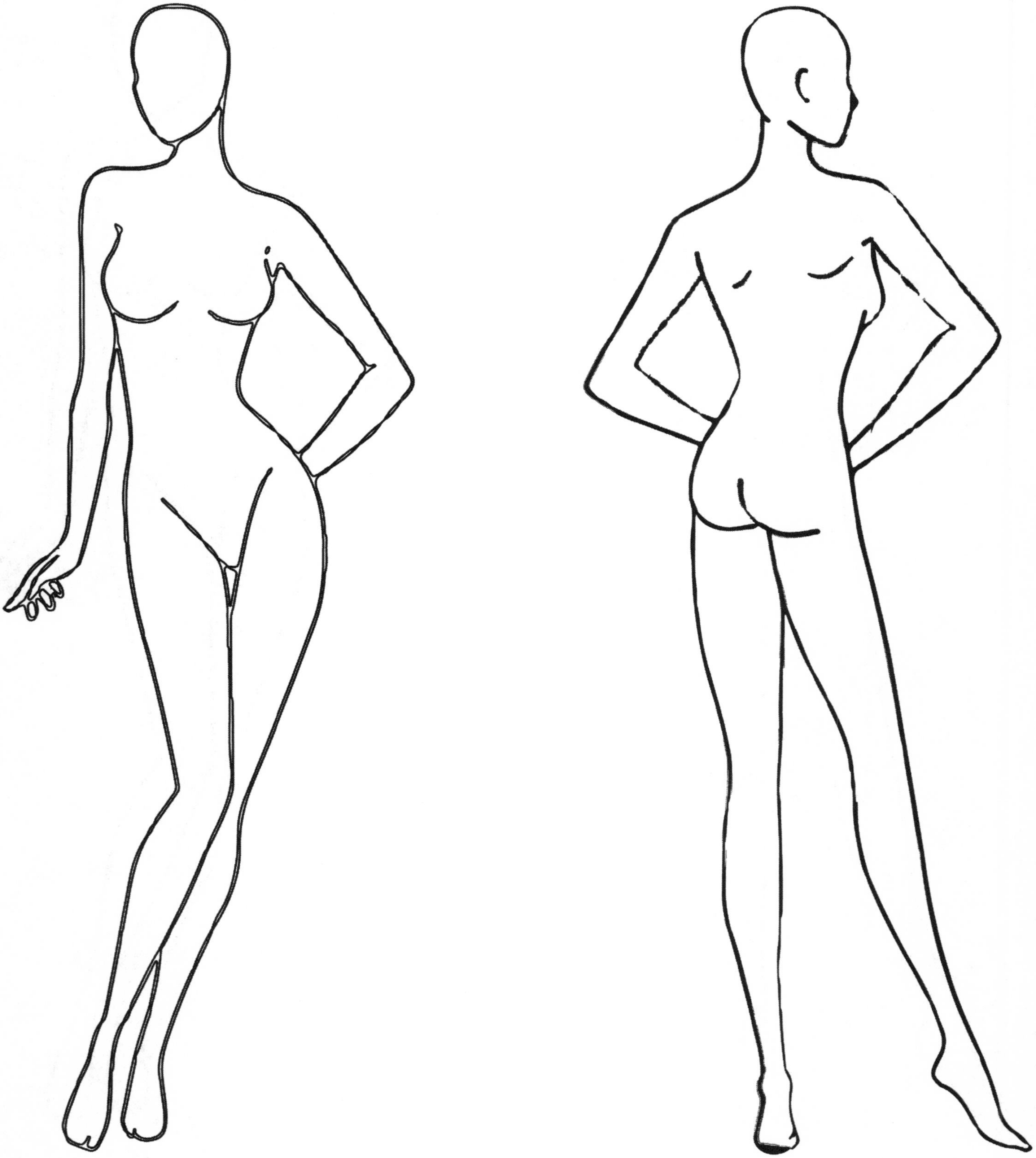

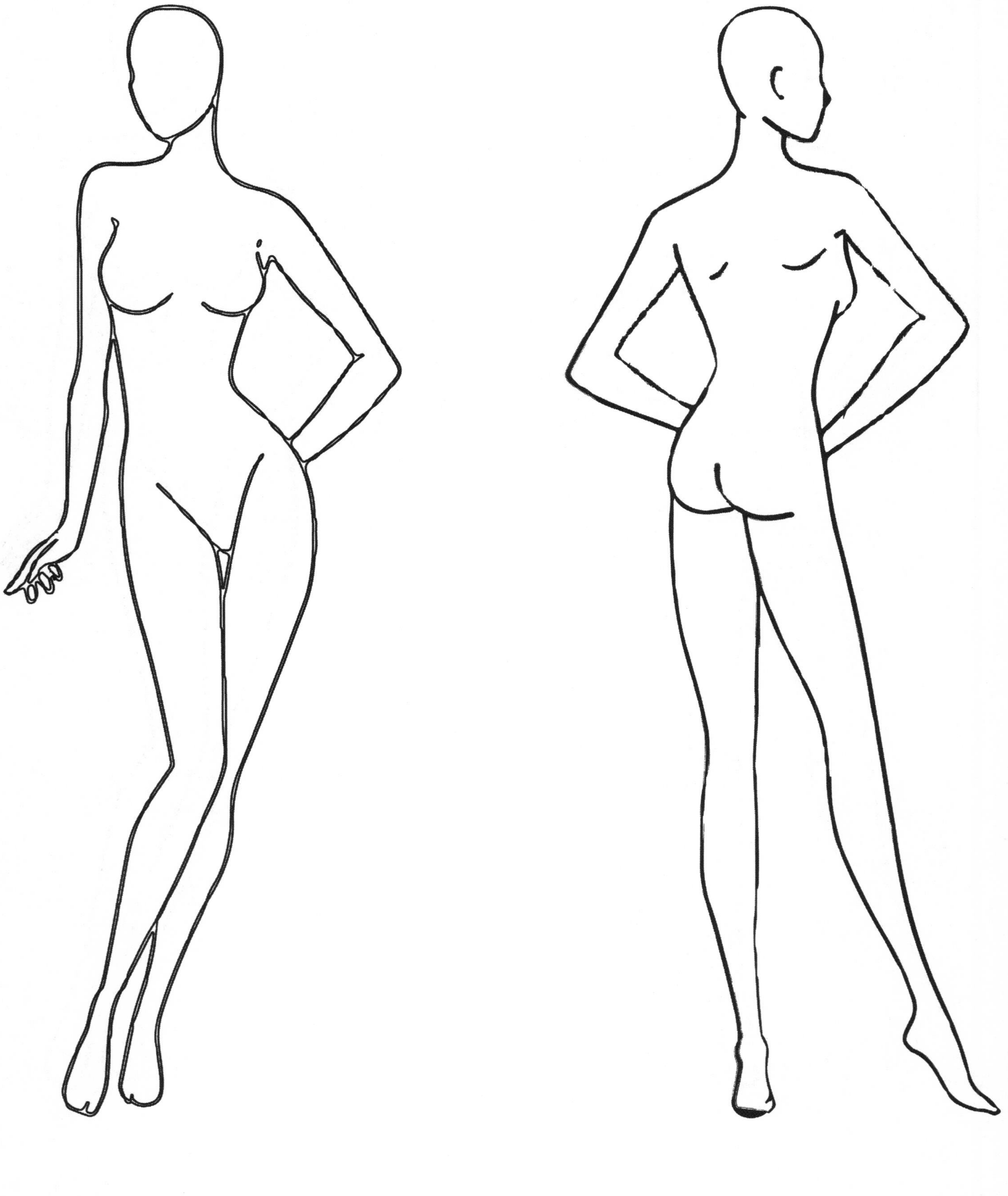

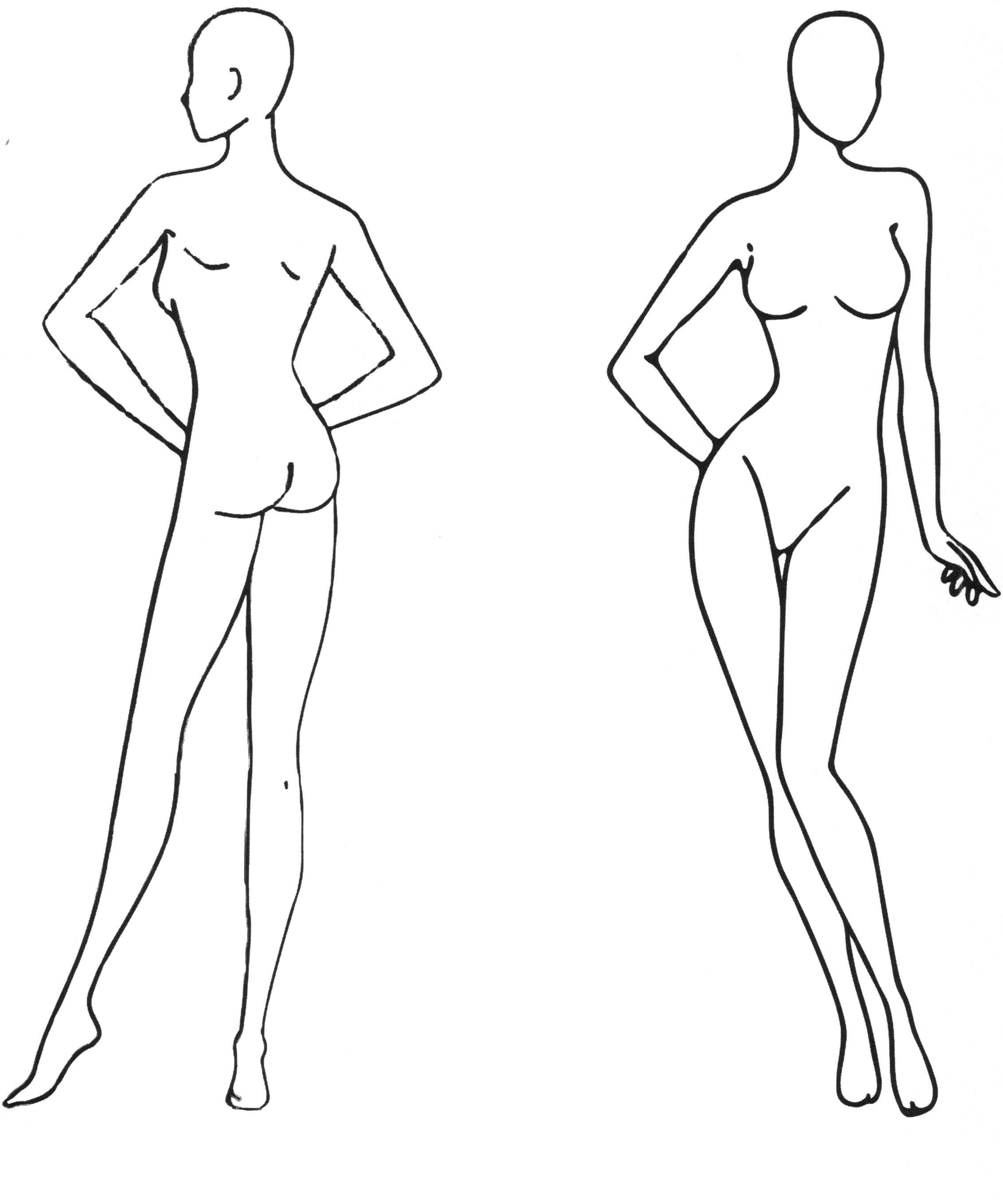

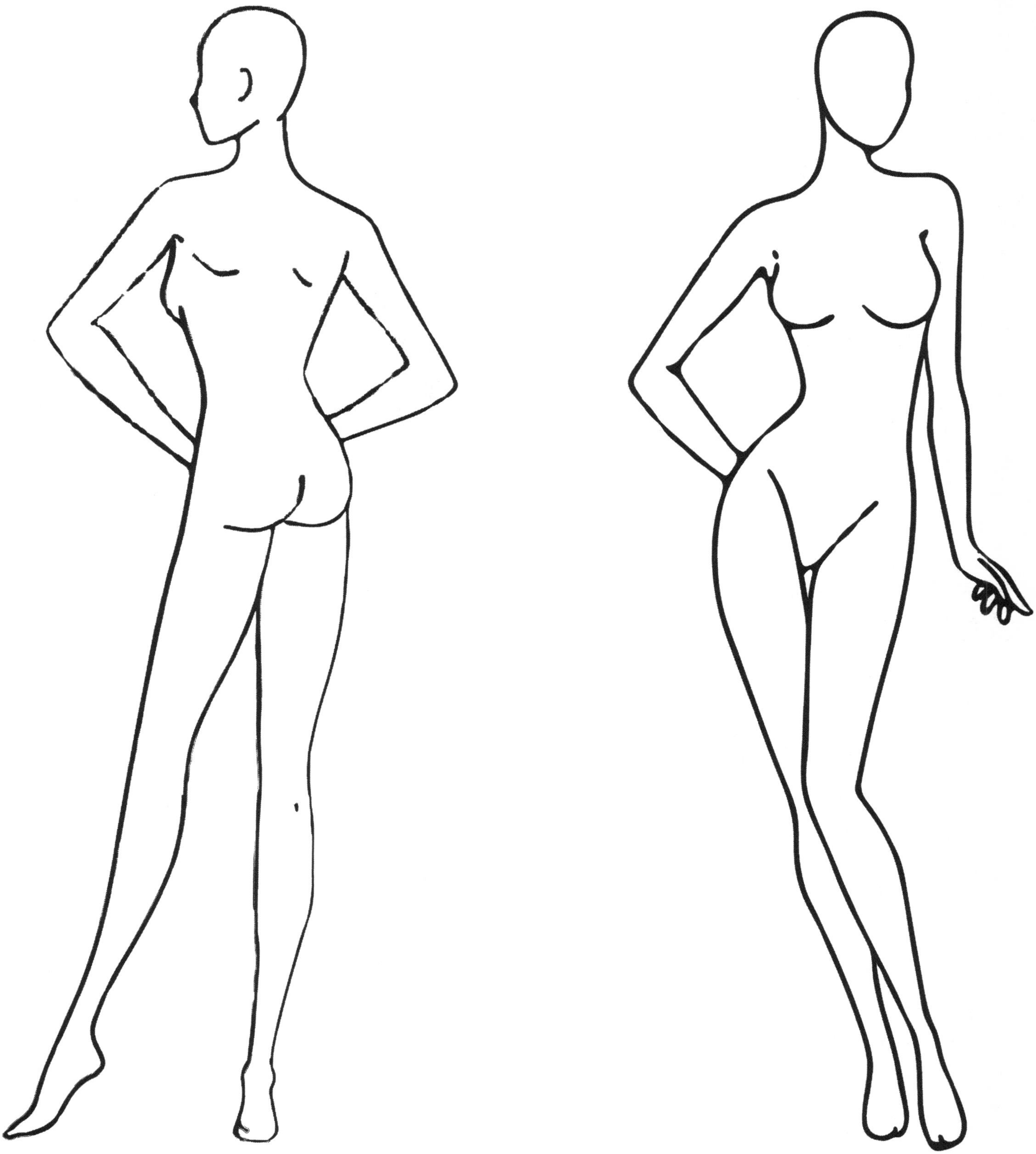

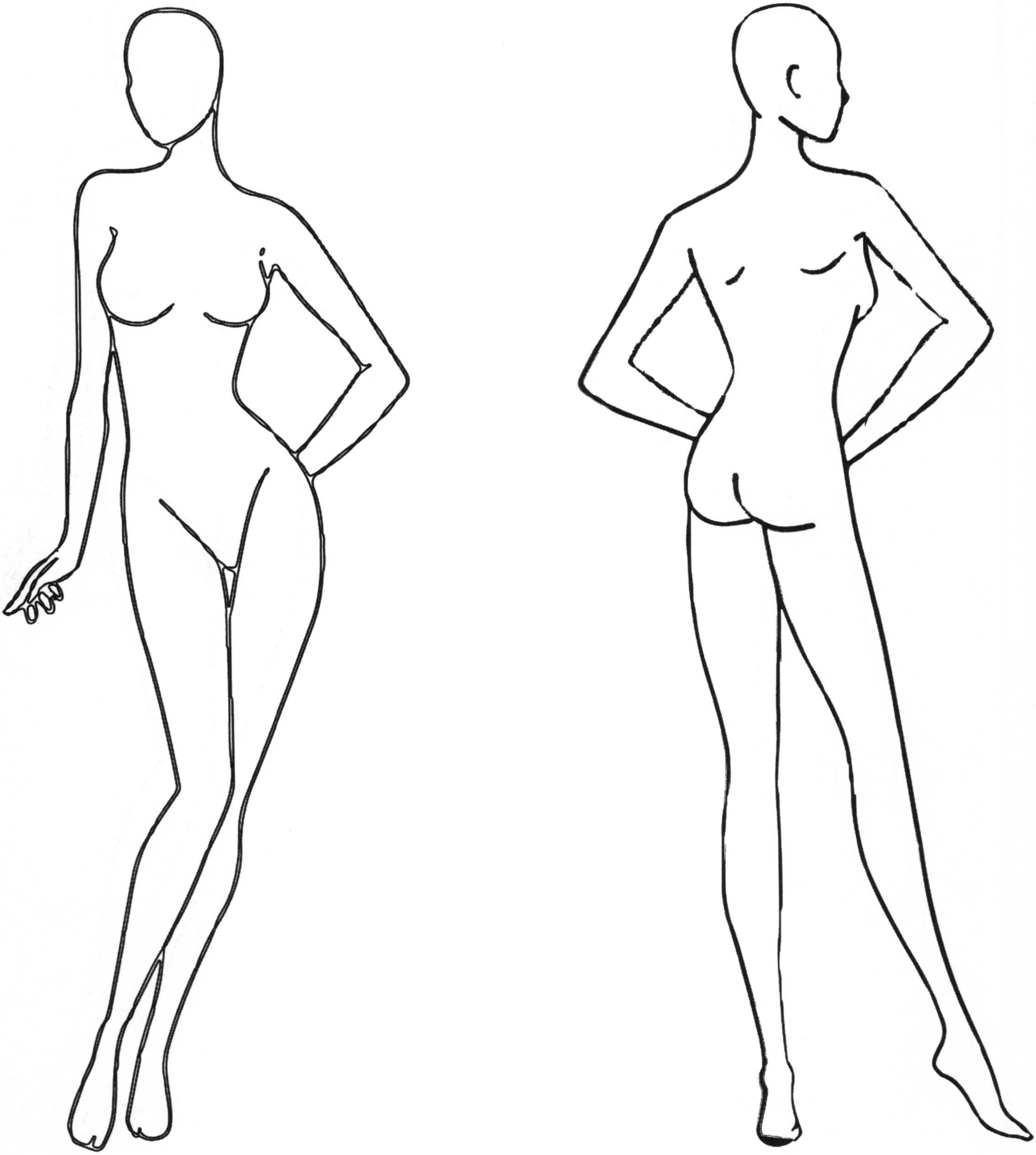

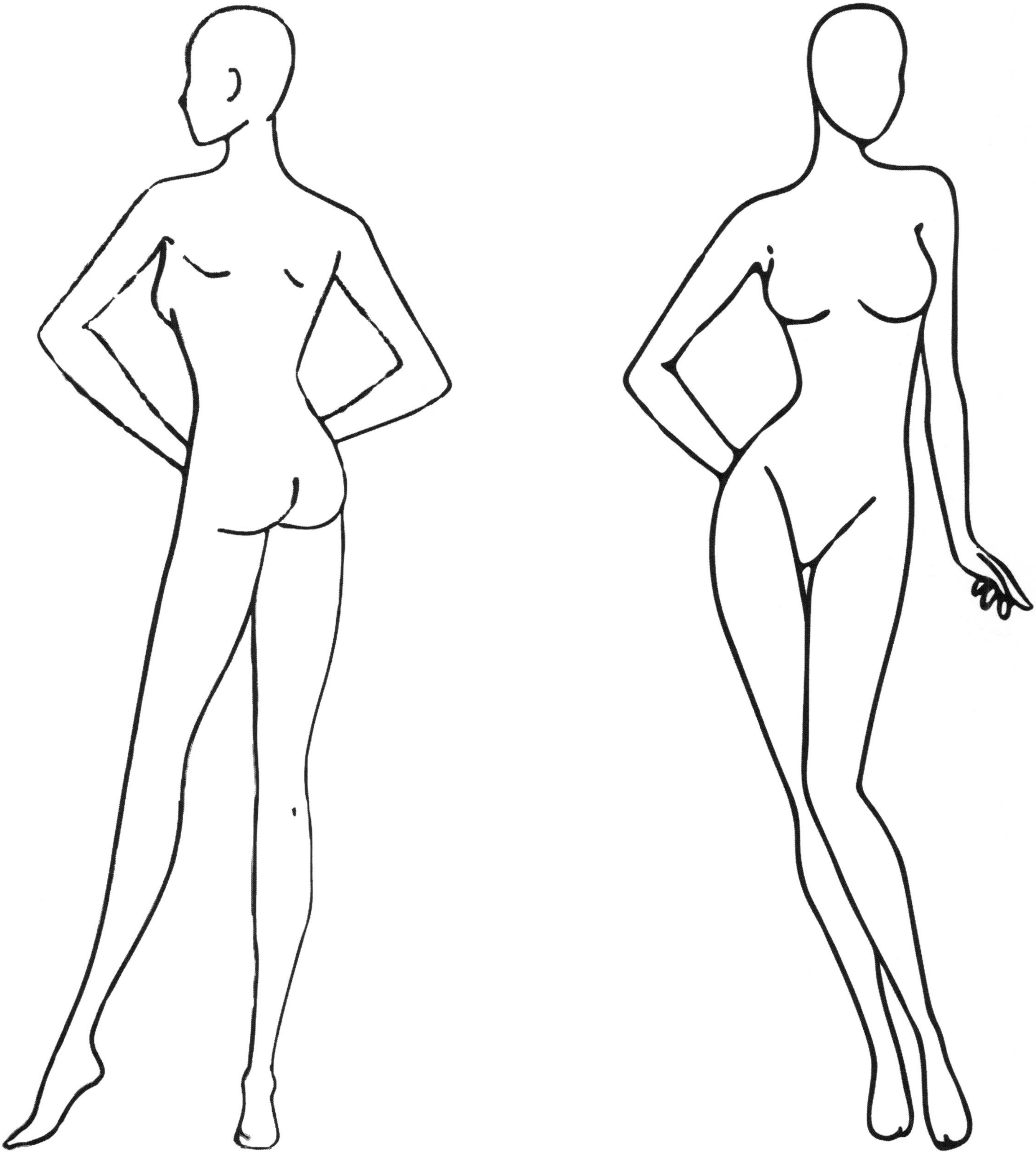

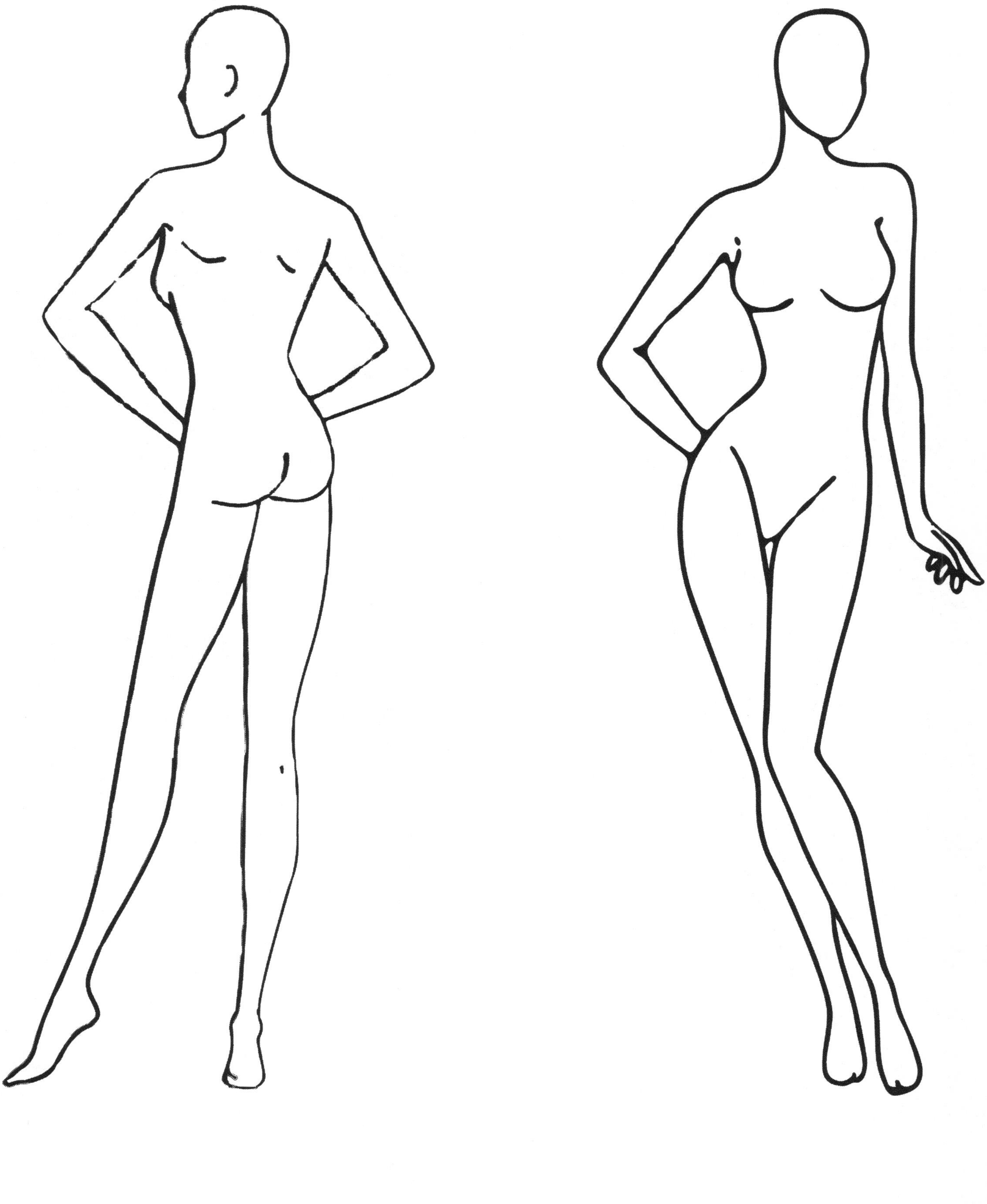

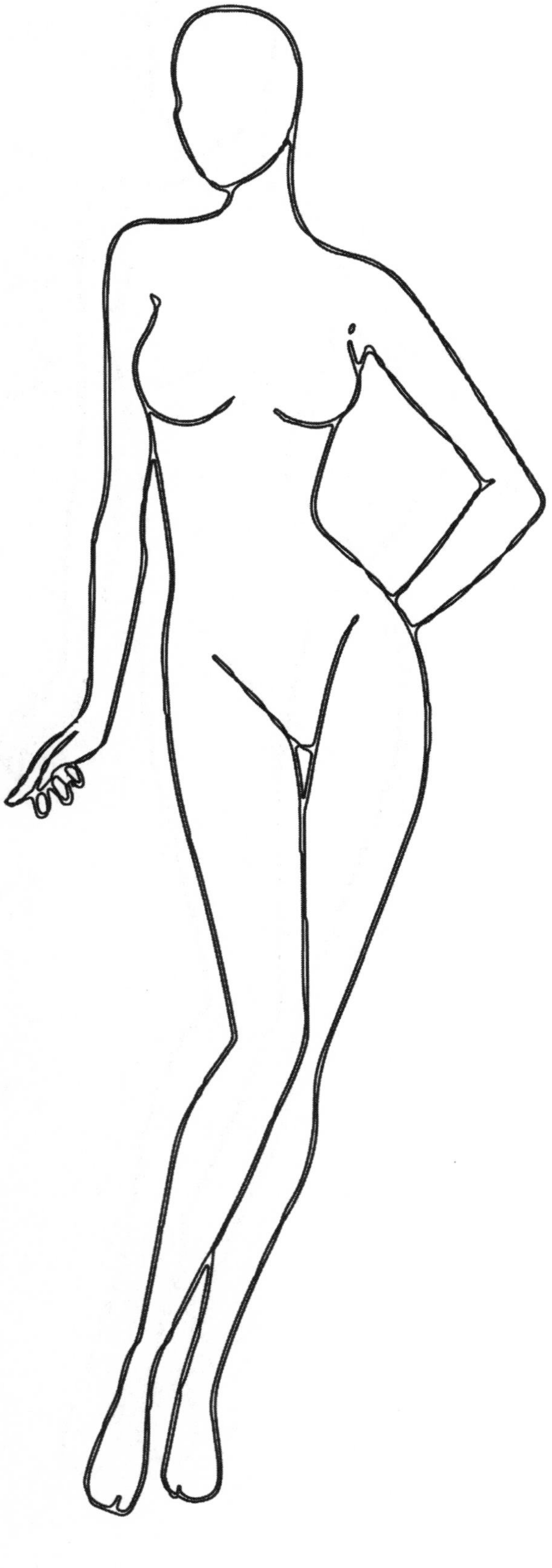

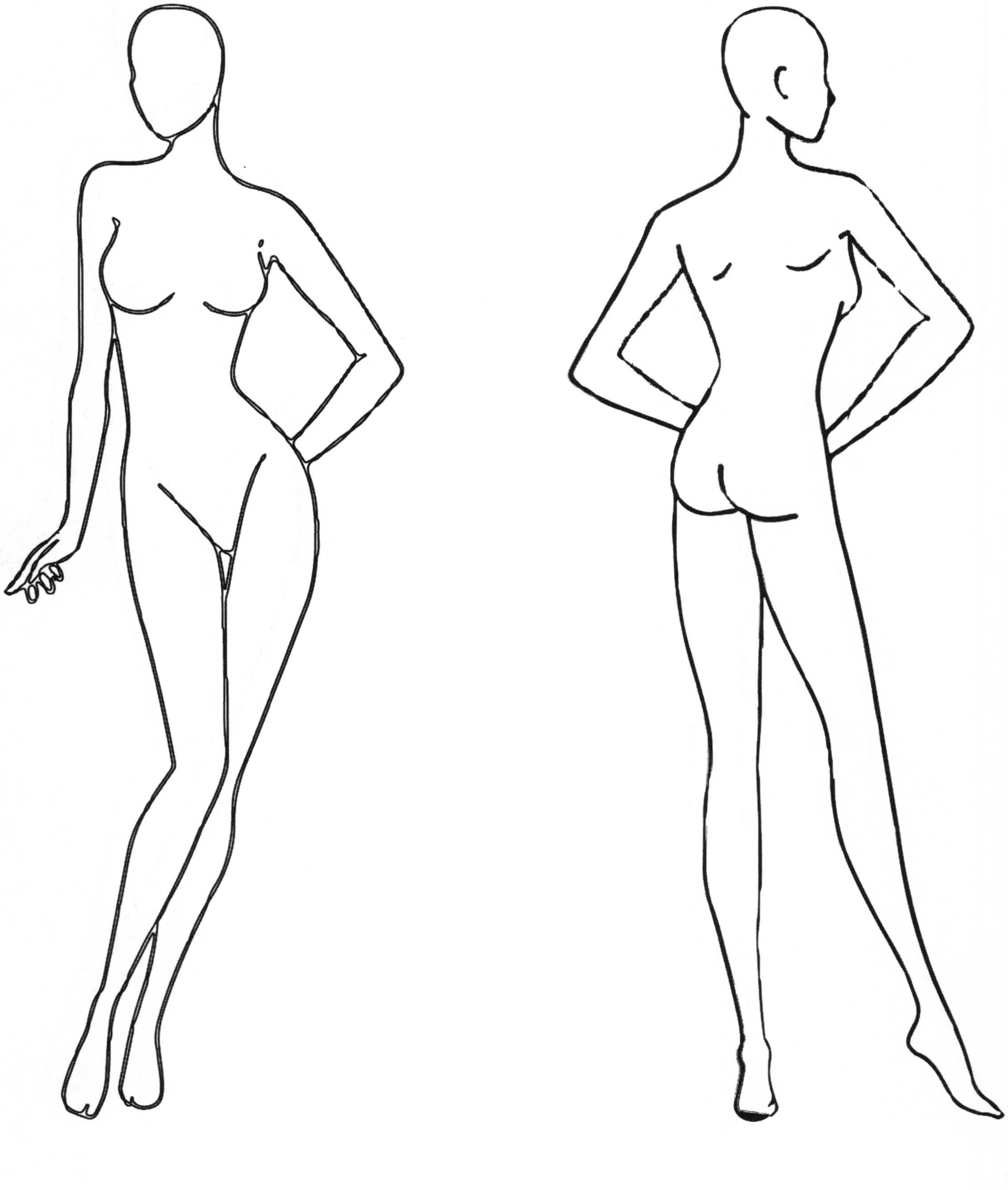

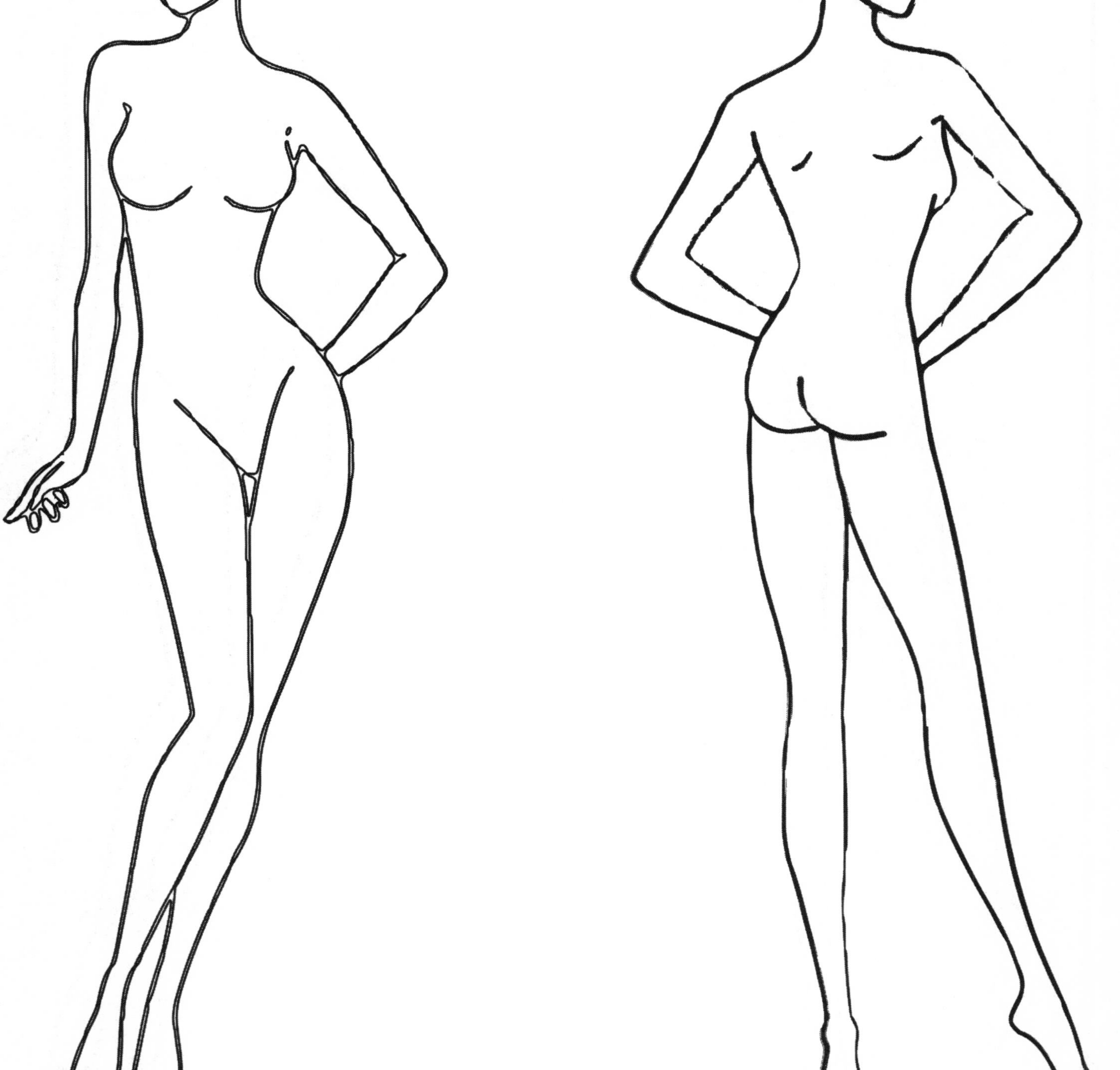

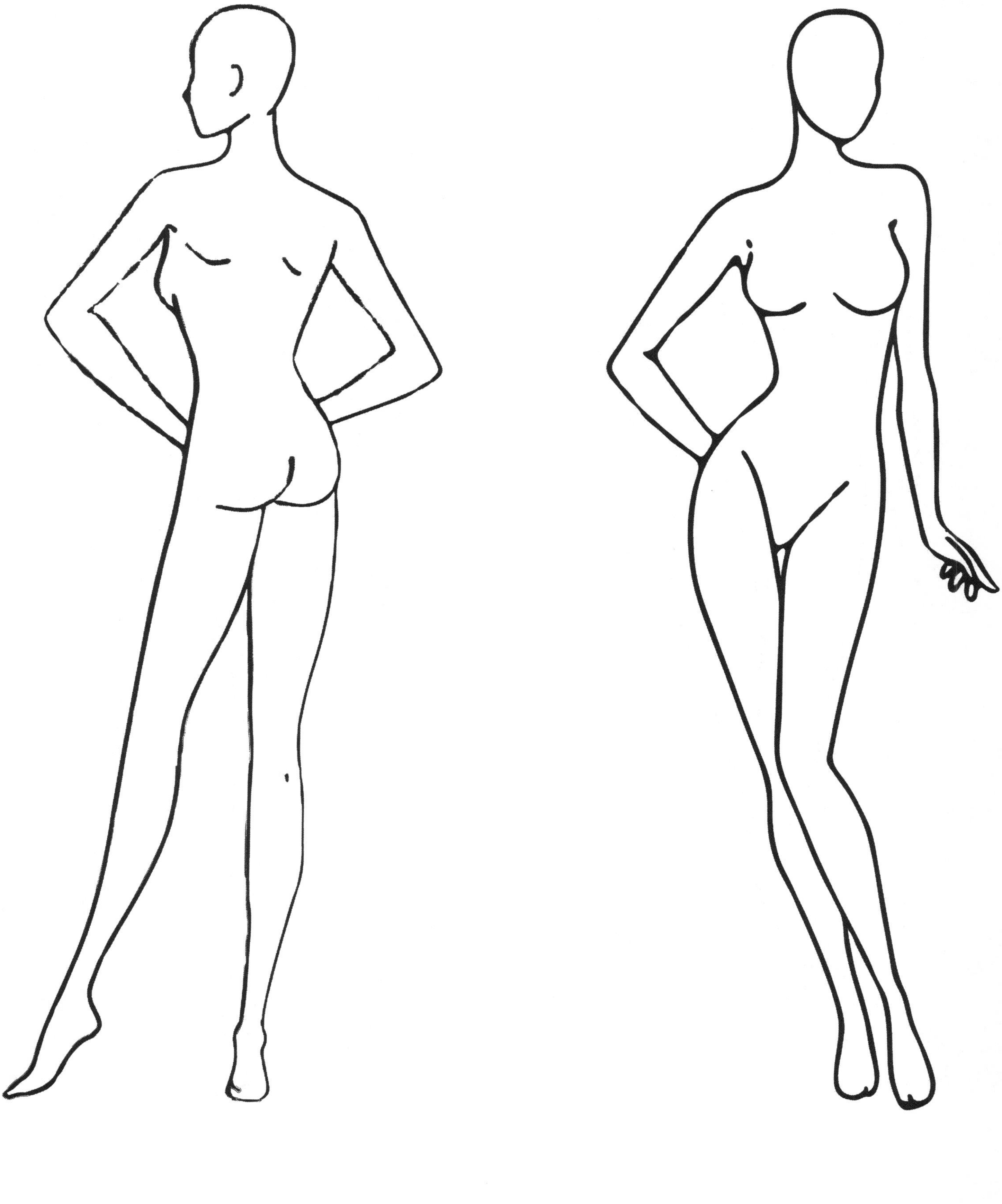

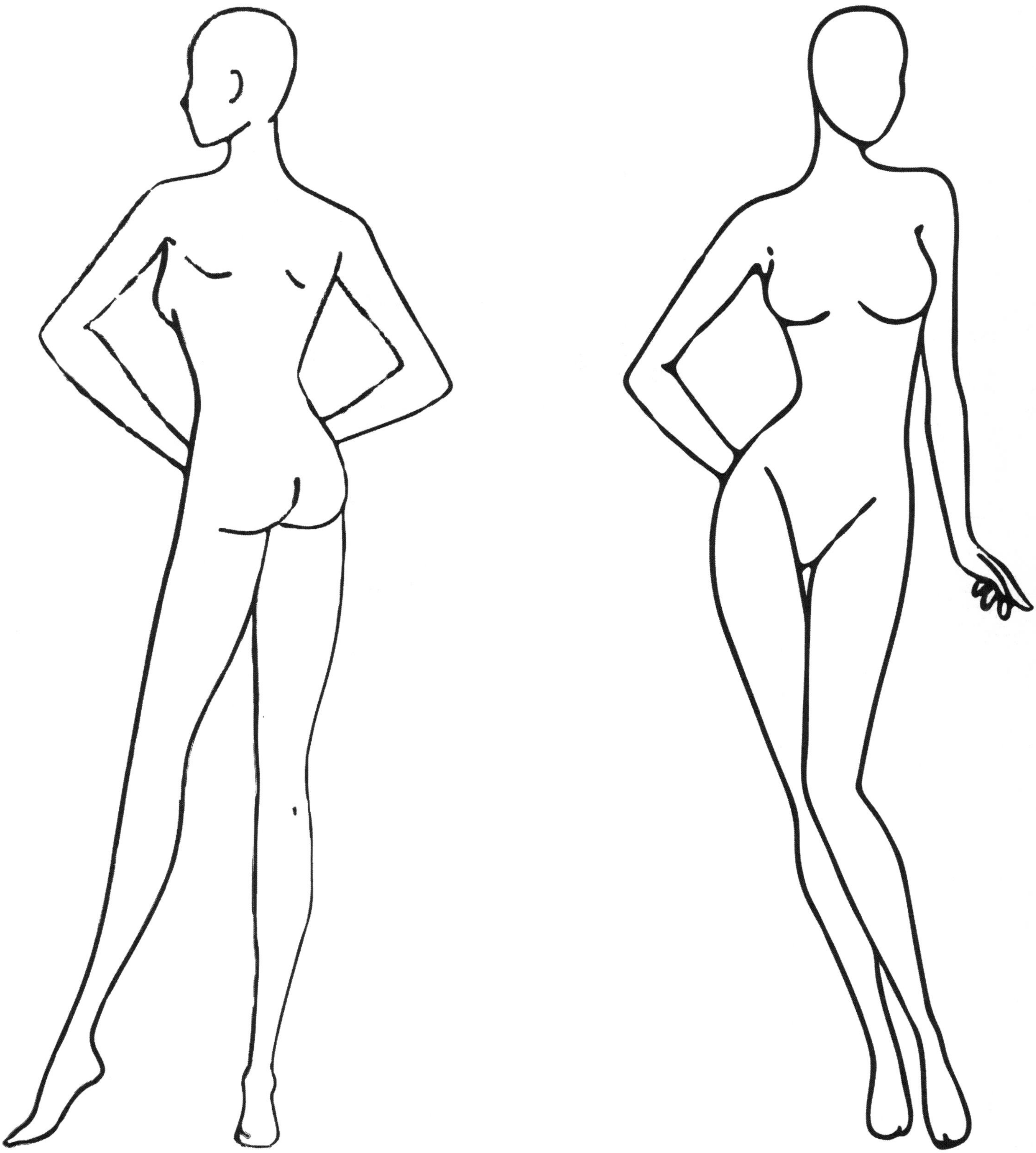

Thank You

15214084R00068

Made in the USA
San Bernardino, CA
16 December 2018